OCS Report
MMS 2009-028

Investigation of Fatality
South Pass Area, South and East Additions, Block 90
Pipeline Right-of-Way OCS-G 26857
18 July 2006

Gulf of Mexico
Off the Louisiana Coast

U.S. Department of the Interior
Minerals Management Service
Gulf of Mexico OCS Regional Office

New Orleans
May 2009

OCS Report
MMS 2009-028

Investigation of Fatality
South Pass, South and East Additions, Block 90
Pipeline Right-of-Way OCS-G 26857
18 July 2006

Gulf of Mexico
Off the Louisiana Coast

Manny Gagliano – Chairman
Mark Malbrue
Melinda Mayes

U.S. Department of the Interior
Minerals Management Service
Gulf of Mexico OCS Regional Office

New Orleans
May 2009

Contents

Abbreviations and Acronyms

CCTV   Closed Circuit Television

CS1   Longitudinal Conveyor System Pipe Joint Position Number 1

CS2   Longitudinal Conveyor System Pipe Joint Position Number 2

CS3   Longitudinal Conveyor System Pipe Joint Position Number 3

GOM   Gulf of Mexico

HSE   Health, Safety, and Environment

JSA   Job Safety Analysis

MMS   Minerals Management Service

OCS   Outer Continental Shelf

PPE   Personal Protective Equipment

QHSE   Quality, Health, Safety, and Environment

RBMO   Rear Bevel Machine Operator

ROW   Right-of-Way

RR4   Ready Rack Pipe Joint Position Number 4

RR5   Ready Rack Pipe Joint Position Number 5

WD 68 JP   West Delta Area, Block 68, JP Platform

Executive Summary

On July 18, 2006, an accident that resulted in one fatality occurred onboard the Allseas Group S.A. (Allseas) pipelay vessel *Lorelay* on Enterprise Field Services, LLC's (Enterprise) Pipeline Right-of-Way (ROW) OCS-G 26857, South Pass Block 90, South and East Additions, Gulf of Mexico, offshore the State of Louisiana.

At approximately 1204 hours, the Stalking Machine Operator was working at his console facing starboard. He heard a loud sound of pipes crashing together, turned around, and saw the Rear Bevel Machine Operator (RBMO) caught between the ends of two joints of pipe. One joint was located on the first pipe joint on the longitudinal conveyor (CS1), and the other joint was located on the fifth pipe joint on the ready rack (RR5). The Stalking Machine Operator immediately went to the RBMO console , which was a few feet away, pushed the emergency stop button, and called for help. The Starboard Spacer heard the call for help. Because the view of the Starboard Spacer was initially blocked by the RBMO's bevel machine, the Starboard Spacer stepped towards the RBMO console, saw the RBMO caught between the ends of two joints of pipe, and shouted to the Bow Bevel Machine Operator to raise the pipe on the ready rack, which the Bow Bevel Machine Operator did. It was necessary to raise the pipe joints on the ready rack to disengage limit switches before the RBMO could be released from the pinch point. The Starboard Spacer then turned the switch on the RBMO console to reverse the pipe trapping the RBMO. As soon as the pipe was reversed, the RBMO fell from between the two joints of pipe to the floor. Within 10 minutes, the RBMO was transferred to the vessel hospital and provided emergency treatment. However, the *Lorelay* vessel physician pronounced him dead at 1300 hours.

There were no eyewitnesses to the accident. Based on information gathered by the investigative panel (panel), the panel concluded that the fatality was caused by the inside pipe conveyor system becoming inadvertently energized, causing uncontrolled pipe movement. The RBMO did not realize that the conveyor system had become energized and was working in the pinch point (between CS1 and RR5) that was in the path of the conveyed pipe. It is unclear how joint CS1 became energized.

Contributing causes identified by the panel include:

1) *Inadequate hazard analyses and failure to implement hazards analyses recommendations.* There was no documentation that a hazard analysis specifically identifying the Bevel Machine Operators as persons at risk had been conducted before the accident. Other hazards analyses conducted before the accident that did not specifically mention the Bevel Machine Operator but that the panel

determined were related to the Bevel Machine Operator's work, did not include the recommendation for a physical barrier to prevent personnel from entering between pipe prep area and conveyor. Therefore the panel concludes that the hazard analyses inadequately identified the hazards in the area where the RBMO was working. In addition, although close-circuit television (CCTV) cameras were installed in the bead stall area as recommended by the hazards analyses, they were not working on the day of the accident. Thus the recommendations of the hazard analyses were also inadequately implemented.

2) Failure to adequately implement and adhere to the recommendations of the Job Safety Analyses (JSA). Although the JSA's indicated that personnel should not walk between pipe joints, the RBMO's hand grinder was stored on a bracket on a wall such that the RBMO had to walk between the pipe joints to obtain the hand grinder. The fact that RBMO would have had to walk between the pipe joints to get his hand grinder, perhaps several times in one shift, may have reinforced the unsafe behavior of working in this pinch point. The JSA also recommended that personnel are to stand to the side of the pipe while grinding. At the time of the accident, the RBMO was working between the pipes.

If these recommendations from the hazards analyses and JSA's had been adhered to, the accident most likely would have been avoided or the severity of the resulting injuries could have been reduced.

Other contributing causes to the accident include an inadequate/poorly written JSA; inadequate supervision; failure of the RBMO to attend safety meetings; and possible inadequate inspection/maintenance of the control panel switch.

Introduction

Authority

On July 18, 2006, at approximately 1204 hours, an accident that resulted in one fatality occurred onboard the Allseas' pipelay vessel *Lorelay* on Enterprise Pipeline ROW OCS-G 26857, South Pass Block 90, South and East Additions, Gulf of Mexico, offshore the State of Louisiana. *(See Attachment 1.)* Pursuant to Section 208, Subsection 22 (d),(e), and (f), of the Outer Continental Shelf (OCS) Lands Act, as amended in 1978, and Department of the Interior Regulations 30 CFR 250, Minerals Management Service (MMS) is required to investigate and prepare a public report of this accident. By memorandum dated August 2, 2006, the following personnel were named to the panel:

> Manny Gagliano, Chairman – Pipeline Section, Field Operations, GOM OCS Region
>
> Mark Malbrue – Lafayette District, Field Operations, GOM OCS Region
>
> Melinda Mayes – Accident Investigation Board, Office of Offshore Regulatory Programs

Procedures

Four MMS representatives visited the accident scene on July 19, 2006, took photographs of the accident scene, and interviewed members of the *Lorelay* crew and Enterprise representatives. Minerals Management Service representatives included Gulf of Mexico Region personnel from the Pipeline Section and the Office of Safety Management. Representatives from Enterprise and Allseas were present to begin conducting their own investigation.

On July 27, 2006, the panel received Allseas' investigative report of the accident from Enterprise. On July 31, 2006, the panel members visited the accident scene to interview *Lorelay* crew members and an Enterprise representative; to observe pipelay operations in progress; and to photograph operations and equipment related to the accident.

By letter dated August 23, 2006, the panel requested the following information from Enterprise:
- Contractual safety requirements imposed on Allseas by Enterprise.
- Minutes from prejob/kickoff meetings between Enterprise and Allseas.
- A written statement from the lead Enterprise representative onboard at the time of the accident.
- "Toolbox Meeting" or other barge safety meeting documentation for the entire job.
- Job Safety Analyses for all positions in the bead stall area.

- Allseas safety policies, programs, and procedures.
- Job descriptions of all personnel in the bead stall area.
- Detailed maintenance and repair reports of the conveyors (inside and outside), pipe elevator, walking beam, and seam rotator systems and controls for the last year.
- Crew manifests that identify dates of crew changes for the entire job.
- Records of precise time of shift change for all personnel working in the bead stall area for the 3 days before the accident and on the day of the accident.
- Autopsy report, including toxicology results, on the deceased.
- Training records for bead stall personnel on duty on the day of the accident.
- *Lorelay* safety records from the previous two jobs, last serious injury occurrence, and last fatality.
- Testing results of limit switch and control system components.
- Mechanical and electrical drawings and schematics of conveyor system including dimensions between rollers, roller heights, and identification of powered rollers, as positioned at the time of the accident.
- Mechanical and electrical drawings of seam rotator and walking beam systems.
- Manufacturer data sheets for the conveyor system, seam rotator, and walking beam components.
- Written statement stating the reason for the installation of the limit switch on the seam rotator and installation date.
- List of RBMO's supervisors and mentors throughout their careers at Allseas and their positions.
- Work history of RBMO at Allseas (positions held and durations in each position).
- Training documentation on RBMO.
- Performance appraisals of the RBMO over the last two years.
- Pipe pull logs for the entire job.
- Barge tension machine logs for the entire day of the accident.
- Barge dynamic positioning logs for the entire day of the accident.
- Precise coordinates in latitude and longitude, pipe station number, and area and block of the *Lorelay* at the time of the accident.
- Barge heading, pitch, and roll data at the time of the accident.
- Weather and sea conditions at the time of the accident.
- *Lorelay* vessel specifications including year built and information on any refurbishments.

- Description of any changes, repairs, or maintenance to the equipment listed below prior to the start of the Independence Trail project and prior to the commencement of laying 24-inch pipe. The descriptions should include the following equipment: conveyor system, walking beam, seam rotator, and other equipment and controls in the bead stall area.

Panel members conducted interviews with personnel from Enterprise's Houston office on September 7, 2006. On August 31, 2006, the panel received Allseas' final investigative report.

Background

On May 16, 2005, Enterprise submitted a request for a pipeline ROW, and installation of a 24-inch diameter gas pipeline, 134 miles in length. The pipeline, known as the Independence Trail Pipeline, is designed to transport gas from Mississippi Canyon Block 920, Platform A (Independence Hub) to West Delta Block 68, Platform JP (WD 68-JP), a right-of-way accessory platform. The water depths along this pipeline route range from 7,940 feet at the Independence Hub to 115 feet at WD 68-JP. On December 21, 2005, MMS granted the ROW and approved the pipeline for installation. Minerals Management Service regulations require that pipelines be designed, installed, operated, maintained, and abandoned to provide safe and pollution-free transportation of fluids in a manner which does not unduly interfere with other uses in the OCS.

Enterprise contracted Allseas, a Swiss-based Company, to lay the Independence Trail Pipeline. The pipeline project involved two Allseas' pipelay vessels and other vessels and barges to support the pipelay operations. Installation of the pipeline began on April 15, 2006, with Allseas' pipelay vessel *Solitaire*. The *Solitaire* installed 0.8 miles of 24-inch steel catenary riser pipe and approximately 85 miles of 24-inch pipe from Independence Hub to the 1,000 feet depth contour, where the end of the pipe was capped and laid on the seafloor. On June 21, 2006, the Allseas' pipelay vessel *Lorelay* picked up the 24-inch gas export pipeline and continued pipelay operations towards WD 68-JP. At the time of the accident, the *Lorelay* had laid 12.7 miles of pipeline and was working in Block 90, South Pass Area, South and East Additions (SP 90), where the water depth is approximately 400 feet.

The *Lorelay* completed laying the Independence Trail Pipeline on August 17, 2006. The end of the pipe was capped and laid on the seafloor in West Delta Block 68, where the JP platform was installed.

Findings

The Pipelay Vessel

The *Lorelay* was built in Germany in 1974 and was converted in The Netherlands in 1986 to be the first pipelay vessel to use full dynamic positioning. *(See Attachment 2.)* The *Lorelay* was registered in the Republic of Panama in 1986. Its overall length is 182.48 meters, and the cargo hold has a maximum capacity of 10,200 tons. The *Lorelay* has the capacity to lay pipe with diameters from 2 inches to 36 inches. Because of the dynamic positioning, the vessel has the capacity for laying pipe in deep water. It has accommodations for up to 216 persons onboard. Crew support facilities include medical facilities with a 3-bed hospital that complies with Norwegian Maritime Directorate (NMD) Regulations.

Joints of pipe being transferred from a barge to the *Lorelay* can be loaded directly into the cargo hold through the aft hatch or onto the main deck outside longitudinal conveyor. This conveyor transports the joints forward into the pipe preparation area. Once in the pipe preparation area, the joints can be conveyed by the inside longitudinal conveyor into the bead stall area, which is where the accident took place, or lowered for storage into the cargo hold via pipe elevators.

The Post-Accident Scene

Pipelay operations were suspended following the accident and the area of the accident was cordoned off. Representatives from Enterprise, Allseas, and MMS arrived on the *Lorelay* within several hours of the accident to examine the scene, take statements and photographs, and interview witnesses before pipeline operations were resumed.

The weather conditions during the investigation were similar to those conditions at which the accident occurred:

- Wind Speed: < 5 knots
- Sea State: Calm
- Swell: Confused, less than 1½ feet
- Vessel Pitch, Roll, and Heave: < 0.5 degrees

The MMS investigators found the accident scene cordoned off and preserved in the state in which the accident occurred. All of the pipe joints on the inside conveyor and ready rack were left as they were at the time of the accident. All of the control panels in the vicinity of the accident were also left as they had been at the time of the accident. Personnel working in the vicinity, at the time of the accident, were made available for interviews and demonstration of their activities. Attachment 3 is a diagram of the overall layout of the bead stall area where the accident occurred, and will be referred to frequently throughout this report. Attachment 4 is a photograph of the accident scene.

The rear bevel machine was mounted on the forth pipe joint on the ready rack (RR4). *(See Attachments 3 and 4.)* A new bevel on the pipe at this location indicated that the RBMO completed beveling and joint preparation operations at RR4. A small amount of metal shavings on the floor under RR4 also indicated that machine beveling operations had been performed. The seam rotator had already rotated the pipe joint at RR5 since the pipe seam was in position for welding, which would take place later in the process. At the time of the accident, the RBMO had moved to RR5 and partially completed initial pipe joint preparation, which involves hand grinding the inside and outside of the pipe. Grinding on the outside of the pipe appeared to be complete. It appeared, at the time of the accident, that the RBMO was grinding on the inside of the pipe. The purpose of the hand grinding was to prepare the end of the pipe joint for the beveling machine, which would clean the pipe of dirt and oxidation to bare metal in preparation for attaching the grounding clamp of the welding electrodes to the pipe.

The RBMO's hand grinder was left on the floor under RR5 where it was dropped at the time of the accident. The grinder appeared to be undamaged. Pipe joint CS1 was within a few feet of RR5. Interviews with the crew indicated that CS1 was left in that position after CS1 was reversed to release the RBMO from between the two pipe ends. The seam rotator was left in an elevated position. According to the Bow Bevel Machine Operator, the seam rotator rollers were used to elevate RR5 such that CS1 could be reversed without moving RR5. This configuration allowed the two pipe joints to be moved apart and the RBMO to be released from between the ends of RR5 and CS1. The walking beam appeared to be lowered and not engaging any pipe joints on the ready rack. The action of the power rollers and unpowered guide rollers functioned normally during the investigation.

The RBMO, Stalking Machine Operator, and Starboard Spacer were in the immediate vicinity when the accident occurred. In addition, the Bow Bevel Machine Operator was working at the bow end of the ready rack. *(See Attachment 3.)* The Starboard Spacer and Bow Bevel Machine Operator were separated from the accident scene by physical barriers. Since the Stalking Machine Operator was closest to the accident scene, he was the first to recognize that the accident occurred. The Stalking Machine Operator was also the first to act by yelling for help and pressing the emergency stop button on the RBMO console. The Starboard Spacer responded to the Stalking Machine Operator shout for help and coordinated with the Bow Bevel Machine Operator to lift RR5 off the conveyor rollers and reverse CS1. Though there were two people in the immediate area at the time of the accident, no one saw the accident occur or the events leading up to the accident. The Stalking Machine Operator and Starboard Spacer, when at their work station, would have normally had their backs to the accident scene. The Starboard Spacer and Bow Bevel Machine Operator normally have their view of the accident scene blocked by pipe on the firing line and ready rack, respectively.

Information gathered in the investigation indicates that the RBMO was standing in the gap between pipe joint positions RR5 and CS1 when the accident occurred. Also, at the time of the accident, a loud noise was reported by all those in the immediate area. There was uncertainty of the origin of the noise. The noise was reported as the typical sound of pipe joints colliding, but louder than usual. Therefore, the noise was most likely the sound of joints of pipe on the inside conveyor colliding with each another. No one could confirm the status of the inside conveyor slots (CS1, CS2, and CS3) immediately prior to the accident. It is unknown whether these slots were filled with pipe immediately before the accident, or if one or more slots were empty and being filled with pipe at the time of the accident. All three pipe slots were filled when MMS investigators first visited the site after the accident. *(See Attachment 5.)*

General Pipelaying Procedures

Attachment 3 shows a plan view of the *Lorelay* and the location of the joint preparation area (bead stall) associated with the accident. Joints of pipe are conveyed through the bead stall area and welded together so that they can be laid on the seafloor. Generally, this process includes:

1) Moving the joints of pipe from the on-deck pipe storage area on the main deck by way of an outside conveyor system to an inside conveyor system that moves the joints of pipe to the ready rack, an area where the ends of the pipe are prepared for welding;

2) Moving the joints of pipe onto the ready rack where the pipe is rotated to place the seam in the proper position, and cleaning the ends of the pipe by hand grinding and beveling with a machine according to exact specifications;

3) Moving the pipe joints from the ready rack to the firing line, where pipe joints are fitted, welded, and field joint coated; then

4) Moving the joints of pipe to the aft of the vessel where they enter the water in a continuous
    string and are eventually laid on the seafloor.

As a joint of pipe is laid on the seafloor, the pipelay vessel advances one pipe joint length, or about 40 feet, along the pipeline route. This is called a "pull." Since the seabed acts as an anchor, the pipe joints on the vessel are advanced down the firing line to make room for the next joint to be fitted and welded by the Stalking Machine Operator, Starboard Spacer, and pipeline welders. While this is proceeding, the RBMO is preparing pipe on the ready rack and operating the inside conveyor to move pipe towards the ready rack.

Each joint of pipe that was being handled at the time of the accident was 40 feet long, 24 inches in diameter, and weighed approximately 9,360 pounds (4.68 tons). Steps 1 and 2 above were the activities that specifically relate to the accident and are described below.

In preparation for welding, joints of pipe are moved from the on-deck pipe storage area onto the outside conveyor system. *(See Attachments 3 and 6.)* The pipe joints are then conveyed to the inside conveyor system. The movements of these two conveyor systems are operated independently by different personnel. When the outside conveyor operator in the pipe storage area sees that there is space available on the inside conveyor system, he operates the outside conveyor system so that joints of pipe are moved from the outside conveyor system to the available spaces on the inside conveyor system. The inside conveyor holds three joints of pipe (CS1, CS2, and CS3), and is operated by the RBMO from his console. *(See Attachments 3 and 7.)* When position RR5 on the ready rack is vacant, the RBMO will advance the pipe on the inside conveyor system to RR5. After the RMBO advances a joint of pipe to RR5, the Bow Bevel Machine Operator operates the seam rotator using the seam rotator rollers to elevate the pipe joint and rotate it so that the pipe joint seam is in the correct position. The joint is lowered upon completion of the seam rotation operation. The RBMO then takes a handheld grinder from the grinder storage location on the wall and uses it to manually clean and smooth the end of the pipe joint where the welding electrode attaches to the pipe.

According to information obtained from interviews, it was routine for the RBMO to stand in the gap between forward-most joint (CS1) on the inside conveyor system and RR5 on the ready rack while using the manual grinder to clean the joint of pipe at RR5. When the RBMO has completed hand grinding at RR5, he moves RR5 to position RR4 on the ready rack by engaging the walking beam using the RBMO console. The walking beam lifts all the pipe joints on the ready rack and shifts them over one joint towards the location of the Stalking Machine Operator. The RBMO then inserts the bevel machine into the end of the pipe at RR4 and turns it on. The bevel machine is operated by the RBMO to bevel the end of the pipe joints to the required specifications. After this beveling is completed, the RBMO removes the bevel machine.

As the RBMO is manually cleaning the pipe and operating the bevel machine at one end of the pipe, the Bow Bevel Machine Operator is conducting the same operations on the bow end of the pipe. All of the controls for moving the pipe joints on the inside conveyor system and the ready rack are controlled by the RBMO from the RBMO console, except for the seam rotator rollers, which are controlled by the Bow Bevel Machine Operator. The RBMO and Bow Bevel Machine Operator are separated by a distance of approximately 40 feet. The RBMO coordinates the pipe joint movements with the Bow Bevel Machine Operator by visual cues from the Bow Bevel Machine Operator or by vocal communication. For example, when the RBMO completes the advancement of a pipe joint from CS1 to RR5, the RBMO signals the Bow Bevel Machine Operator that it is safe to operate the seam rotator rollers. Upon completion of the seam rotation operations, the Bow Bevel Machine Operator notifies the RBMO that the operation is complete.

Equipment and Controls

The conveyor systems and ready rack are designed to operate by moving joints of pipe into and through the bead stall area, as needed, while at the same time preventing unintended movements of the pipe joints. More specific details of the equipment and controls that govern pipe joint movement in the area where the accident occurred are discussed below.

Outside Conveyor

As noted above, the outside conveyor system is used to move pipe joints from the pipe storage area to the inside conveyor system. It is operated by a crew member in the pipe storage area and is independent from the movement of the inside conveyor, which is operated by the RBMO. The crew member in the pipe storage area operates a simple push button to control the outside conveyor system. When he presses the control button, pipe joints on the outside conveyor move forward one joint. The crew member will activate the outside conveyor when he sees that there is an available space on the inside conveyor at position CS3. It is possible for the pipe storage crew member to mistakenly advance a joint of pipe from CS4 when there is already a joint of pipe on the inside conveyor at CS3.

Inside Conveyor

11

The inside conveyor transports pipe joints to the ready rack. The RBMO activates the inside conveyor system with the forward and reverse controller, a spring loaded twist switch that is on the same control panel as the walking beam joystick controls. This control panel is 8 feet away from the nearest pipe joint on the conveyor system. *(See Attachments 3 and 7.)* The twist switch is twisted to the left to advance pipe joints (forward) on the conveyor system towards the ready rack, and to the right to reverse pipe joints on the conveyor system away from the ready rack. If the operator releases his grip on the twist switch, it is designed to automatically spring back to the neutral position. This ensures that the pipe joints on the inside conveyor and RR5 come to a stop when RR5 is filled.

Seam Rotator

Once a joint of pipe has been moved onto RR5, it must be lifted and rotated so that the longitudinal pipe joint seam is in the proper position. The seam rotator is operated by the Bow Bevel Machine Operator. When the seam rotator is activated, the pipe joint at RR5 is lifted from the forward moving rollers on the ready rack onto a set of seam rollers that will rotate the pipe.

Walking Beam

The walking beam moves pipe joints on the ready rack in a transverse direction towards the line-up station . The walking beam is controlled by a joystick on the RBMO's control panel. *(See Attachment 7.)* To operate the walking beam, the RBMO moves the joystick to the "up" position. This lifts all five pipe joints from the ready rack. The RBMO then moves the ready rack joints laterally towards the line-up station by moving the joystick to the "left." Once the end joint is in the line-up station, the RBMO lowers the five pipe joints by moving the joystick to the "down" position. The RBMO resets the walking beam to the start position by moving the joystick to the "right." Photographs taken by MMS personnel, during the on site investigation immediately after the accident, show that a small copper tube had been added to the joystick to extend the length of the joystick. *(See Attachment 8.)* The Allseas' investigative report indicates that this was done because the RMBO control panel was installed on a relatively low pedestal requiring personnel to bend down to operate it.

Limit Switches

To control the movement of pipe joints and to prevent them from moving unintentionally, two limit switches are installed on the inside conveyor and the ready rack. When the switch on the RBMO console is twisted to the left, the pipe joints on the inside conveyor advance one joint forward. Limit Switch 1 is installed at the bow end of the RR5 position on the ready rack. When the twist switch is moved to the left, the joint at CS1 moves onto the ready rack and stops when it comes in contact with limit switch 2, whether or not the operator releases the switch to neutral. limit switch-1 senses the presence of a pipe joint on the ready rack in position RR5. If a pipe joint is present at RR5 engaging limit switch 1, the twist switch will not activate the conveyor system, thus preventing the advancement of pipe joints towards the ready rack. The reverse function on the conveyor system still works normally with limit switch 1 engaged so that a pipe joint at CS1 can be moved back a short distance if it is too close to the pipe joint at RR5. Limit Switch 1 can be defeated with a spring loaded override button on the top of the control panel. *(See Attachment 8.)* In order to activate the override feature, the operator is required to use both hands simultaneously, one on the twist switch and one on the override button. During normal pipelay operations, the override button is used to advance pipe if excess gaps between pipe joints occur on the inside conveyor system while there is a joint in the RR5 position. In this case, to prevent the joint in position RR5 from further advancing and falling off the bow end of the ready rack, the RR5 joint must be lifted off the power rollers while the joints on the inside conveyor system are advanced. The joint at RR5 can be lifted in two ways, either by using the walking beam on the ready rack or by using the seam rotator rollers.

When the seam rotator rollers are used to lift the pipe at RR5, limit switch 1 is disengaged. To prevent pipe joints from moving while the pipe joint is lifted by the seam rotator, Limit Switch 2 is installed in the lifting arm of the seam rotator. *(See Attachment 3.)* Limit Switch 2 is designed to be engaged before limit switch 1 is disengaged, thus preventing any forward movement of pipe joints on the inside conveyor system when the pipe is lifted onto the seam rollers.

If the walking beam is used to lift the pipe joint at RR5 while the other joints on the conveyor system are advanced, it is possible to defeat both RR5 limit switches. This would allow automatic advancement of all pipe joints on the conveyor system until they either collide with the slightly raised RR5 joint, or until the emergency stop button is activated on the control panel by the operator. It is noted by Allseas, in their investigation, that limit switch 1 is defeated when the pipe joint in position RR5 is lifted approximately 2.5 centimeters off rollers by the walking beam. In this situation, limit switch 2 would also not be engaged, thus allowing the pipe on the inside conveyor to move forward. There were no indicator lights or sounds to indicate that limit switches were or were not properly engaged.

The following tests of limit switch' and the inside conveyor system were conducted:
 1) During the initial investigation on July 18, 2006, representatives from Enterprise, Allseas, and

13

MMS witnessed a test of the limit switch' and longitudinal RBMO systems. All of the switches and systems performed normally during this test. Allseas conducted further tests as part of its investigation and did find that the inside conveyor actuator switch did occasionally stick in the forward (left) position.

2) During the initial investigation on July 18, 2006, representatives from Enterprise, Allseas, and MMS witnessed a test in which the outside conveyor pipe at CS4 collided with the pipe joint at position CS3. The purpose was to determine if this could generate enough momentum to propagate motion all the way to position CS1. Joint CS3 moved less than 2 inches in all tests and caused no movement in joints CS2 or CS1. It was determined that there was little chance that

such an operation could generate enough momentum to effect a movement of a pipe joint in position CS1.

1) Independent Maritime Consulting (Gulf) Ltd. conducted tests on the limit switch'. Results from the tests showed that the operation of the inside conveyor selector switch felt sluggish and sometimes stuck in the "on" position when it was turned left. Dirt was found in the actuator upon disassembly. A piece inside the actuator was cracked.

RBMO and Bow Bevel Machine Operator Controls
Controls for the operation of the inside conveyor and the walking beam are located on the RBMO's console. *(See Attachments 3 and 7.)* This console is located approximately 8 feet from the location of the accident.

Control for the seam rotator rollers is located at the Bow Bevel Machine Operator's station. *(See Attachment 3.)* The Bow Bevel Machine Operator has the capability of raising and lowering the seam rotator rollers and the pipe joint in position RR5, and then using these rollers to axially rotate the pipe joint in position RR5. The purpose of the seam roller is to rotate the pipe joint in position RR5 such that the longitudinal weld seam has the correct orientation for weld preparation and fitting. The RBMO is not capable of operating the seam rotator rollers at his control console.

Personnel and Job Tasks
The pipeline lay vessel *Lorelay* averages about 203 personnel onboard the vessel. The crew works a rotation schedule of 2 months on/2 months off. Individual crew members' rotation schedules were

staggered so that there would not be a complete crew turnover at any one time. The production crew in the bead stall area worked 12-hour rotating shifts.

According to interviews with Allseas' personnel, there were three production crew members in the immediate area of the accident, the RBMO, Stalking Machine Operator, and Starboard Spacer. In addition, the Bow Bevel Machine Operator was working at the bow end of the ready rack. *(See Attachment 3.)* Allseas' documentation indicates that the front and end crews in the bead stall area usually change shifts between 1130 hours and 1200 hours. However, there is no record kept of the precise time the shift changes occur. Interviews with Allseas' personnel indicated that shift changes were staggered so that production would not have to be shut down during the shift change. Individuals in each position agreed with each other on the specific time, within an half-hour window, when they would change shifts.

The RBMO and Bow Bevel Machine Operator had similar job responsibilities but at different ends of each pipe joint. The job description and qualifications for both positions, as described in one Allseas' document, are noted below.

Rear and Bow Bevel Machine Operator (BMO) Job Tasks
- Set up beveling machine(s) to cut pipe ends to specifications laid out in welding procedure(s).
- Monitor pipe ends closely to ensure specifications are adhered to.
- Monitor number of cutting inserts/seats used per shift.
- Dispose of metal shavings properly.
- Perform normal day-to-day maintenance on beveling machines.

None of the job tasks listed in the BMO's job description included the hand grinding/buffing operations or moving of pipe either along the inside conveyor, on the ready rack, or with the seam rotator rollers. Interviews with Allseas' personnel indicated that there was no specific training for the BMO's job tasks other than on-the-job training. Interviews also indicated that the RBMO and Bow Bevel Machine Operator would change positions periodically under no formal schedule.

BMO qualifications listed in the Allseas' documentation included:
- Minimum one year experience or to have completed Allseas' in-house training course.
- Must speak English.
- Completion of external safety/trade training as per company's training matrix (no training matrix was provided by company).

15

Rear Bevel Machine Operator Job Experience, Training, and Performance

At the time of the accident, the deceased was working as the RMBO. The RBMO had several years of experience in both the RBMO and Bow Bevel Machine Operator positions on the *Lorelay*. This was the RBMO's first day in this position since the start of this project 27 days earlier. Prior to this, the RBMO had worked at the Bow Bevel Machine Operator position. However, he had extensive experience in both the bow and rear BMO positions. Employment records show that he had been employed by Allseas since June 1, 1986, and had worked on the *Lorelay* for most of that time. He had worked 16 years on the *Lorelay* as a Rigger, then 4 years as a BMO. In his 4 years as BMO, about 3½ years were spent on the *Lorelay* and 6 months on other Allseas' vessels. At the time of the accident, both BMO's had been on the *Lorelay* for 1 month; the Stalking Machine Operator had been on the vessel 3 weeks; and the Starboard Spacer for 7 weeks.

The RBMO had the following training certificates:

- March 4, 2004 – Safe Crane Operation (Overhead Gantry) Participation Certificate competence. This certification expired on February 4, 2006.
- February 4, 2006 – Further Offshore, Emergency Response, Basic Safety and Contingency Refresher Course; Refresher Offshore Safety Introduction and Emergency Response Training, including Airpocket. A refresher course was required to be completed on or before February 4, 2008.

The team reviewed Allseas' job performance evaluation for the RBMO. The RMBO was evaluated numerically on nine different job elements: experience, skill, productivity, English, work quality, accuracy, safety, flexibility, and initiative. A weighting factor ranging from 2-5 was also assigned to each job element. The highest weighted element was safety (5); the next highest elements were skill, productivity, and work quality (each weighted 4). From the information provided, it appears that the performance rating scale ranged from 1-10 for each of these elements. However, the panel was not able to interpret the RBMO's evaluation because a key to the rating scale was not provided.

Supervision

There were supervisors, crew members, and a client representative who performed activities that would periodically bring them into the immediate area of the accident. However, according to interviews, none were in the area at the time of the accident. The Chief Engineer and the Allseas' Quality Control Inspector did not acknowledge that the RBMO would work in the gap between RR5 and CS1. Crew members interviewed, including the Starboard Spacer, Stalking Machine Operator, and the Enterprise Chief Inspector , did not specifically observe the RBMO working in the gap prior to the accident.

The Quality Control Inspector is responsible for monitoring pipe joint tallies as each joint passes through the firing line. The Safety Officer is responsible for monitoring activities with regard to safety, health, and environment. This included such activities as conducting daily rounds, documenting appropriate safety briefings, helping with corrective actions, providing training when required, assisting risk assessment teams, etc. The Allseas' safety officer in charge, at the time of the accident, indicated that he would usually visit the area where the accident occurred at least once per shift. He arrived onboard the *Lorelay* on the day of the accident and had not yet visited the area where the accident occurred.

Procedures, Hazards Analyses, and Job Safety Analyses

The team examined Allseas' written risk assessments (hazards analyses) and JSA's prepared for *Lorelay* operations associated with activities in the area where the accident occurred. The documentation provided to the panel included three hazards analyses, each listing specific hazards of the operation and precautions that could be taken to address the hazards. The three analyses examined by the panel rated the hazards as moderately low risk, with the risk being reduced to low if the precautions recommended in the analysis were in place. The hazards analyses also indicated whether or not the recommended precaution(s) had been put in place. Below is a summary of the 3 hazard analyses examined by the panel.

Hazard 1

Process/Operation: Horizontal transport from storage rack to preparation rack.

Equipment: Storage rack, preparation rack, stopping rods, roller box lines.

Hazard: Entanglement.

Persons at risk: Rigger Foreman/Riggers

.Precautions in place as of the date of the assessment conducted on November 14, 2004:

- No personnel in between storage rack and preparation rack.
- Stop rods installed to prevent uncontrolled rolling of loose pipe.
- Limited number of personnel in area.

17

- Personnel briefed/instructed on non-routine activity.

Precautions added to the hazard analysis and in place at the time of the assessment conducted on August 25, 2006 (post accident):

- Those listed above (as of November 14, 2004).
- Barrier in place to prevent personnel entering between pipe prep area and conveyor.

Hazard 2

Process/Operation: Horizontal transport of pipe from preparation rack to "foreship."

Equipment: Preparation rack, stopping rods, roller box lines, stop switch, walking beams.

Hazard: Uncontrolled movement (swinging) of pipe.

Persons at risk: Rigger Foreman/Riggers.

Precautions in place at the time of the assessments conducted on November 14, 2004 and on August 25, 2006 (post accident):

- Operations stop when vessel movement excessive, noted as "common practice."
- Stop switch installed to prevent pipe moving further forward.
- Stop rods installed to prevent uncontrolled rolling of loose pipe.
- Limited number of personnel in area.
- Personnel briefed/instructed on non-routine activity.

Hazard 3

Process Operation: Pipe beveling and buffing.

Equipment: Beveling machines.

Hazard: Entrapment/Crush from moving pipes.

Persons at risk: BMO, Rigger Foreman, Riggers, Welders, Welders Helpers.

Precautions put in place as of the date of the assessment conducted on July 22, 2006 (post accident):

- Restricted areas, close-circuit (CCTV) cameras, procedures for pipe moving operations.

Precautions in place as of August 20, 2006 (post incident):

- Those listed above (as of July 22,,2006).
- Ensure all barriers at incoming pipe conveyor are installed in place (restricted area).
- No buffing works on incoming pipe conveyor.

The documentation provided shows that analyses for Hazards 1 and 2 were conducted before the accident in 2004. These two analyses were recommended for review in one year. The panel received no documentation indicating that reviews were conducted in 2005. Although these analyses do not specifically identify the BMO's as persons at risk from these hazards, the description of the equipment and operations appear to include those that would involve the BMO's. Reviews of Hazard 1 and 2 were also conducted after the accident. In the post-accident review of Hazard 1, a new recommendation for putting a physical barrier between the "pipe prep area and the conveyor" was added to the analysis and put in place. No changes were made to the analysis for Hazard 2.

An analysis of Hazard 3 was conducted just a few days after the accident. The documentation of this analysis specifically included the BMO's as being persons at risk from this hazard. That analysis recommended: 1) Ensure that all barriers at the incoming pipe conveyor are installed in place (restricted area) and 2) No buffing work allowed on the incoming pipe conveyor. The analysis indicated that neither of these precautions was in place at that time. A review of this Hazard Analysis was also conducted a month later. At that time, the two precautions above were identified as being in place. The panel received no documentation that an analysis of Hazard 3 was conducted before the accident.

Another precaution recommended in the analysis for Hazard 3, conducted on July 22, 2006 was the installation of CCTV cameras. However, panel interviews found that at the time of the accident, the cameras were not working in the bead stall area.

The team also reviewed two JSA's, dated November 28, 2005, that addressed BMO tasks related to the accident. Job Safety Analysis 1 (JSA1) addressed activities related to bevel machine operation. Job Safety Analysis 2 (JSA2) addressed the use of the seam roller and pipe transfer arm (walking beam). The Allseas' JSA form includes a check list of 18 pieces of safety equipment that could potentially be required for the task. Barricades are listed on the form, but were not recommended in either JSA.

Overall, the two JSA's were not clearly written. The two JSA's overlap in that JSA1 includes the operations described in JSA2. Most steps listed in the JSA's do not indicate who is performing the function. Job tasks for both the RBMO and Bow Bevel Machine Operator include lifting/moving pipe. Neither JSA distinguishes which BMO (or both) are responsible for each discrete task in the task sequence. There is also no information describing how/when the BMO's were to communicate with each other to ensure their pipe lifting/moving tasks were coordinated and completed safely.

In addition, the sequences of task steps are vague or poorly defined, and important steps in the task sequences are not listed. For example, before the RBMO would start to hand grind/buff the end of the pipe, he would have to retrieve the hand grinder. This step was not listed in the JSA, but was an important step from a job safety point of view since the RBMO's hand grinder was located on the wall and required him to walk between a pinch point (between pipe joints CS1 and RR5) on the inside conveyor system. Also, neither the lifting of the pipe onto the seam rotator rollers nor rotating the pipe were mentioned in either JSA.

Most of the job sequence steps in JSA1 are written as precautions to be taken rather than as discrete steps in the work process. For example, one step states, "Go under pipe, not between pipe." Since this step does not state where the worker is moving from/to, the RBMO may not have understood the significance of this precaution in his work area and, hence, did not perceive the associated danger. The wording of the recommendation to reduce the hazard of this step is similar to the wording of the step itself and states, "Don't walk between pipes."

An example of a poorly defined or vague work step in JSA1 states, "BMO operations whilst machine in rotation mode." There is no description of what these "operations" are. Another poorly defined work step in this JSA states, "BMO operating pipe on rollers." Looking at the recommendation to reduce the hazards for this step, it appears that the step refers to the pipe being advanced on the longitudinal conveyor, rather than the seam rotator rollers. However, this is not clear from the task sequence.

At the time of the accident, the limit switches were the only physical/mechanical barriers protecting the RBMO from getting caught between pipes on the longitudinal conveyor. However, the operations of these limit switches are not well integrated into the JSA's. Job Safety Analysis 1 does state that, after operating the walking beam, one should ensure that the limit switches are engaged. Job Safety Analysis 2, which also discusses operation of the walking beam, does not mention this limit switch. Neither JSA mentions the operation of the limit switch that stops the movement of the pipe on the longitudinal conveyor. In addition, neither JSA discusses how the operation of the limit switch is affected when the pipe is lifted onto the seam rollers.

Since there was no direct observation or oversight of the process being conducted in the bead stall area at the time of the accident, the panel could not determine if the job task sequence and all precautions listed in the JSA were being carried out.

Recommendations that the JSA's included to reduce the hazard of being caught or struck by pipe include:

- Wait until the pipe comes to a complete stop before entering area.
- BMO carries out visual check down conveyor rollers.
- Ensure that rotational rollers are down before commencing pipe rack movement.
- "Stand side-on to pipe when grinding."
- "Go under pipe, not between pipe."
- Don't walk between pipe.
- One operator to control the process.
- Non-essential personnel stay clear.

During interviews with the *Lorelay* crew, the team discovered that it was routine for RBMO's to conduct the grinding and buffing operations while standing in the pinch point between pipe joints CS1 and RR5. Also, from observing the pipe conveyor system, the team determined that it would be very difficult for the RBMO to go under the pipe while retrieving the hand grinder from the wall bracket.

Corrective Actions Taken by Allseas

The following corrective actions were immediately implemented on the pipelay vessel *Lorelay* after the accident:

- A safety barrier was placed in the area where the RBMO was crushed to prevent personnel from walking or working between the pipe joints at CS1 and RR5.
- A selector switch that controls the inside conveyor system, along with two limit switches, were replaced with new ones. The old switches were shipped out to a lab for further review.
- Allseas evaluated and updated their hazards analyses in the conveyor system and ready rack areas.
- The storage location of the RBMO grinder was moved from the starboard wall to a location on the near side of the conveyor system. This eliminated the need for the RBMO to walk in the gap between RR5 and CS1 to retrieve the grinder

.

Safety Management

Pipeline Installation Agreement

On April 29, 2005, an offshore pipeline installation agreement was formulated between Enterprise (Company) and Allseas (Contractor) that covered the scope of work and details of the Independence Trail Gas Export Pipeline Project from Mississippi Canyon 920 to WD-68 on the Gulf of Mexico OCS. Included in this document were the Company's expectations of the Contractor regarding health and safety. The following points are included in the health and safety section of the agreement:

- Contractor shall at all times maintain discipline and good order among its employees and those of its subcontractors, vendors, or agents.
- Contractor shall adequately instruct all its employees, and those of its subcontractors or agents, in the use of safety equipment and proper work procedures for the purpose of doing everything reasonably possible to protect against personal injury and damage to equipment.
- Contractor shall establish safety rules and procedures in accordance with Exhibit H (described below).
- Contractor shall require that all its employees, and those of its subcontractors or agents, observe such safety rules and regulations, as well as any that may be issued by Company, and any safety regulations issued by agencies of any government having jurisdiction over the work.
- Contractor shall take all reasonable measures necessary to provide safe working conditions, including posting danger signs and other warnings against hazards, promulgating safety regulations, and notifying owners and users of adjacent utilities or facilities.
- Contractor shall furnish the Company promptly with a report of each accident and "near miss" within 1 hour of the incident or occurrence, and shall notify all relevant agencies, as required by law.
- Contractor shall conduct safety drills aboard all vessels for all personnel.
- Company may, at any time, conduct audits and inspections of Company's safety procedures prior to or during performance of any portion of the work.

The health and safety section also prohibited alcoholic beverages, firearms, and illegal drugs from being on any vessel. Smoking/open flames were also prohibited except in Contractor-designated areas. In addition, this section requires the Contractor to carry out the Federal drug and alcohol testing requirements at 49 CFR 199.

Pipeline Installation Agreement, Exhibit H
As noted above, the Contractor was to establish safety rules and procedures in accordance with Exhibit H. Policy statements that were included in Exhibit H include the following:

- Comply with the letter and spirit of all applicable health and safety regulations and laws and to maintain a self-monitoring audit program to ensure continuing compliance.
- Assist all levels of government in the promulgation and amendment of health and safety laws, codes, and rules in order to achieve regulations that are: 1) based on scientific fact; and 2) economically and operationally feasible.
- Assume that the expense of health and safety compliance is a legitimate cost of doing business in a modern society.
- Manage operations with diligence, with an awareness that the goal is zero incidence of situations or events which endanger personnel, equipment, and materials.
- Hold each line manager accountable for compliance with the Company's policy within his or her area of responsibility.
- Encourage all employees to become involved in the safety and accident prevention system and to adopt safe working conditions.
- Train employees to be aware of the impact of their assignments as it relates to health and safety, and to assume responsibility for implementing the policy on the level of their applicable assignment.
- Encourage employees to report immediately any unsafe work condition, unsafe work practice, or hazard to a responsible supervisor.
- Regard health and safety review as routine when evaluating contractors, vendors, existing facilities or properties under consideration for employment, acquisition, or sale.
- Ensure that all vendors, contractors and their subcontractors possess, at a minimum, similar management polices and that these entities diligently and consistently enforce accident prevention, health and safety procedures and practices.
- Establish, at a minimum, a health and safety procedures and guidelines manual, which shall be made available to every Company employee.

Exhibit H also included a section that provided an overview of safe work practices. The topics addressed in that overview are listed below.

- Purpose and Scope.
- Commitment.
- Contractor Responsibility.
- Facility Boarding and Departing Requirements.
- Prohibitions.
- Search and Seizure.

- Personal Safety and Personal Protective Equipment (PPE).

- Personal Flotation Devices.

- Over-Water Transfers.

- Man Overboard.

- Belts, Lifelines, and Lanyards.

- Transportation.

- Operations (which includes an overview of personnel safety work rules).

- Smoking.

- Regulatory Standards.

- Reporting Accidents and Hazards.

- Equipment Operation.

- Electrical.

- Housekeeping.

- Fire Prevention and Firefighting.

- Medical Services and First Aid.

- Hazardous Materials.

- Records and Recordkeeping.

- Visitors.

- Hot Work.

- Confined Space Entry.

- Lockout/Tag out.

- Simultaneous Operations.

- Classified Areas.

Allseas' Quality, Health, Safety, and Environment Managemet System Plan

The objective of safe working procedures, in Allseas' Quality, Health, Safety, and Environment (QHSE) Management System Plan, was to provide practical guidance on safety, health, and environmental protection. Generally, Allseas' safety policies and procedures are specified in writing. Allseas' corporate safety policy (General Introduction to Allseas' QHSE Management System) and Health, Safety, and Environment (HSE) Project Plan were attached to the pipeline installation agreement.

Allseas' QHSE Plan included a corporate policy statement; health and safety objectives; HSE responsibilities and activities; performance monitoring; and information about audits and inspections. Allseas' corporate policy statement indicates, "Allseas Health and Safety Policy and Objectives have been established to provide a safe and healthy working environment for the company's employees, its subcontractors and others affected by its activities. The policy is generally issued to all personnel working offshore via Allseas Offshore Safety Booklet or through the line manager to key personnel." Allseas' HSE project objectives were listed as follows:

- Where applicable, the policies as contained in Exhibit H of the contract will be implemented.
- Good HSE performance will not be compromised by commercial or schedule pressures.
- Onshore and offshore personnel are made aware of the importance of HSE within this project.
- Reportable incidents are investigated to prevent recurrence.
- Discharges and emissions are kept to a minimum through all phases of the project.
- All solid wastes are disposed in an approved and auditable manner.

Allseas' vessel safety statistics between 2001 and 2005 are documented in its QHSE Management Plan. These statistics indicate that during this period there were 0 fatalities, 21 lost time injuries , and 50 medical treatment cases. Allseas' definition of an loss time injury is a work-related injury which prevents an employee from continuing the job he/she was performing prior to the injury up to a period of three shifts. Allseas' definition of medical treatment cases is based on the definition given by the Occupational Safety and Health Administration (OSHA), USA regulations. In 2005, the frequency rates for loss time injurys, and for all recordable cases, were .45 and 2.09, respectively, for every 200,000 hours worked. Recordable cases include all medical treatment cases, loss time injury's, and fatalities. In addition, Allseas' vessel safety performance statistics indicate that in 2005 there were 42 near misses (an undesired event which, under slightly difference conditions, could have resulted in damage to personnel, equipment, or the environment). The number of near misses that occurred in 2005 was the second highest during the 5-year period, and was 11 more than the 5-year average.

In the past Enterprise has utilized Allseas on several occasions. Management has indicated that there was a series of project-related meetings conducted to discuss safety and technical procedures of the job. Prior to the operation, the Independence Trail initial kickoff meeting was conducted on April 12, 2006. It covered the overview of the project that was being conducted when the pipelay vessel *Solitaire* was in use. When the project mobilized offshore, a second kickoff meeting was performed prior to the *Lorelay* portion of the operation. During interviews with Enterprise personnel, the panel was told that Enterprise thinks highly of Allseas' operations, including its management, organization, procedures, equipment, and personnel. Enterprise personnel indicated that Allseas conducted numerous projects for them in the offshore deepwater over the years. Enterprise also indicated that Allseas displayed an outstanding safety record during these pipeline laying operations.

In order to verify a contractor's performance, Enterprise reviewed the Contractor's safety records. In this case, Enterprise did not monitor Allseas on a monthly basis because of its affiliations with Allseas. Two projects prior to this operation were the last time Allseas' records had been reviewed by Enterprise. During the previous projects, Enterprise did not have any accidents or near misses that raised any safety concerns. During the pipeline installation, Enterprise used the *Solitaire* to lay the deeper section of the 134-mile pipeline from the Hub Facility (8,000 feet to 950 feet of water depth). The *Lorelay* came in on the shallow water depth, and laid the remaining pipeline sections to the West Delta Area (115 feet of water).

The communication between Enterprise and Allseas was managed by each company's Project Manager on a daily basis. In the field operation, Enterprise's Inspection Crew monitored the operation, which has a Chief Inspector that supervises the crew. The Chief Inspector is Enterprise's main communication link to the Project Manager. The Chief Inspector reported to the Project Manager, on a daily basis, any operational and safety issues, if there were any. Both Enterprise's and Allseas' Project Managers were able to visit the vessels to witness various portions of the project. Prior to the time of the accident, no issues or concerns were identified during the pipeline operation. The Chief Inspector strongly indicated that there were no language barriers.

During the course of the operation, personnel were expected to work safely, which was to be accomplished by conducting regular safety meetings with crew members. The HSE Committee conducted various types of meetings, such as the HSE Committee Meeting, the Pre-shift Meeting, and the Toolbox Meetings. According to Allseas' OHSE Management System, biweekly, daily, and other unscheduled meetings were to be conducted on the vessel. Records indicated that there were a total of 61 HSE, Pre-shift, and Toolbox meetings conducted on the vessel from July through August 2006. In the observations of the safety meeting documentation, the RBMO did not appear to be in attendance at any of the safety meetings. Other meetings conducted during the pipeline laying operation were the JSA meetings, which also did not have any records of his attendance. The Chief Inspector indicated that safety walkabouts were conducted weekly. Safety walkabouts were general safety inspections conducted by a safety team. This team consisted of the Chief Inspector, Superintendent, Barge
Captain, and Chief Engineer. If any unsafe conditions or concerns existed, they were immediately reported to the vessel's Safety Officer. The Chief Inspector strongly complimented Allseas for running a clean vessel free from any hazards.

Conclusions

The Accident

According to the written witness statement from the Captain of the *Lorelay*, the *Lorelay* was installing 24-inch pipeline in SP 90. The weather conditions during the accident were as follows:

- Wind Speed: < 5 knots
- Sea State: Calm
- Swell: Confused, less than 1½ feet
- Vessel Pitch, Roll, and Heave: < 0.5 degrees

Although there were no witnesses to the accident itself, the team has identified the following sequence of events as a likely scenario, based on the evidence gathered during the investigation. Immediately prior to the accident, there was a pipe "pull" where the vessel advanced along the pipeline route exactly one pipe joint. Since the seabed acts as an anchor, the pipe joints on the vessel advanced down the firing line to make room for the next joint to be stalked on. This was the first pipe pull after the shift change that normally occurred between 1130 hours and 1200 hours. Rather than have all crew members change shift at once, crew changes occur in a staggered fashion over this time period.

The RBMO had begun his shift at approximately 1125 hours. At least three joints of pipe had been prepared on the ready rack by the preceding RBMO before the shift change. Based on the pull logs, the RBMO completed the preparation of two joints of pipe since the beginning of his shift and was working on the third pipe joint when the accident occurred.

Standing at the conveyor console, the RBMO used the joystick to lift the walking beam, which laterally advanced the five joints of pipe on the ready rack. Still at the console, he then activated the pipe conveyor system to advance a joint of pipe onto the open slot in position RR5 on the ready rack.

The Bow Bevel Machine Operator had begun his shift at approximately 1155 hours. At this point, the Bow Bevel Machine Operator lifted the pipe at RR5 with the seam roller to rotate the pipe into the proper position. Upon completion of the seam roller, the Bow Bevel Machine Operator then lowered RR5. About the same time, the RBMO moved from his console to the ready rack and inserted the bevel machine into the end of the pipe joint at ready rack position RR4. At the same time, the Bow

Bevel Machine Operator was in the process of doing the same thing at his end of the pipe at ready rack position RR4.

Next, the RBMO approached the gap between the pipe joint in position RR5 and the pipe on the conveyor system in position CS1. The RBMO walked in the gap between the two joints of pipe at RR5 and CS1 to get his grinder hanging on the wall. He then positioned himself in the gap to begin hand grinding the end of the pipe joint at RR5 in preparation for installation of the welding electrode ground clamp.

Pipe joint CS1 became energized and advanced towards RR5 while RR5 remained stationary. The investigative panel has not been able to identify a logical explanation of what caused CS1 to begin moving.

A loud noise of pipe crashing together was heard by all personnel in the ready rack; bead stall; welding stall numbers 2, 3, and 4; and along the conveyor system. The RBMO was crushed between CS1 and RR5. The Stalking Machine Operator immediately turned around and saw the RBMO crushed between the two pipe joints. The Stalking Machine Operator went to the RBMO's console and pressed the emergency stop button. The lead spacer also approached the control panel and yelled to the Bow Bevel Machine Operator to lift RR5 (with the seam roller) so that the conveyor control switch on the RBMO console could be operated to reverse the pipe joint at CS1 and release the RBMO from between the joints of pipe. The Bow Bevel Machine Operator was in the process of unbinding the machine and backing it out of the pipe joint when he heard a yell from the Starboard Spacer to lift the pipe. The Bow Bevel Machine Operator lifted the pipe with the seam roller and the Starboard Spacer reversed the pipe at CS1. Upon being released from between the two pipe joints, the RBMO fell to the ground.

According to the Bow Bevel Machine Operator, he was working on his first pipe bevel of his shift when the accident occurred. When his bevel machine was inserted in the first joint of his shift, it was misaligned with the pipe joint. This misalignment caused the bevel machine to bind. Immediately prior and during the time of the accident, the Bow Bevel Machine Operator was preoccupied with the malfunctioning bow bevel machine.

Cause

The fatality was caused by the inside conveyor system becoming inadvertently energized, causing uncontrolled pipe movement. The responsible conveyor operator (RBMO) did not realize that the conveyor system had become energized and was working in an area in the path of the conveyed pipe that was a pinch point. The pipe on the conveyor system (CS1) struck the RBMO in the back and pinched him between that pipe joint and the stationary joint of pipe that was in the fifth position on the ready rack (RR5).

It is unclear how joint CS1 became energized while the RBMO was well out of reach of the only control console that operates the inside conveyor system. Interviews with the *Lorelay* crew indicated that no other personnel were seen in the area within reach of the control console when the accident occurred.

It is also unclear why the pipe joint RR5 was not energized when CS1 was energized. Under normal operation, RR5 would have been conveyed in the same direction and at the same speed as CS1 since the conveyor rollers act in unison.

Probable Causes

Since there were no eyewitnesses of the accident when it occurred, the team was unable to develop a definitive scenario as to exactly how the accident happened. All conclusions are based on evidence at the accident scene, documentations provided by the contractor and ROW holder, and personal interviews.

Scenarios for the Uncontrolled Movement of Pipe

There are three basic scenarios that could have caused a pipe joint(s) on the conveyor system to move and trap the RBMO: 1) External forces impacted the pipe on the inside conveyor system; 2) Failure or malfunction of the equipment/controls; and 3) Improper or inadvertent operation of the equipment/controls.

1) *External Force.* External force has been ruled an unlikely cause of the accident. The weight of each pipe joint and the configuration of rollers on the conveyor system prevent movement by the outside forces possible surrounding the time of the accident. The outside forces considered were the momentum of pipe on the outside conveyor system and vessel motion. The outside conveyor system is independent of the inside conveyor system. It is possible for joints of pipe on the outside conveyor system to collide with joints of pipe on the inside conveyor. It was determined by the investigative panel that momentum, that could have been

29

induced by pipe on the outside conveyor system, was insufficient to propel joint CS3 more than one inch. Therefore, momentum of the pipe on the external conveyor system was deemed insufficient to cause the accident.

Vessel motion was also ruled out as a cause for the accident since the seas were calm and there were no reports of unusual weather conditions or vessel motions at the time of the accident.

2)   *Mechanical Failure or Malfunction.* Mechanical failure or malfunction of the conveyor components have been considered. Failures include the limit switch' and operator panel switches controlling the inside conveyor rollers, power roller motors, and roller control system.

The conveyor control schematics, limit switch', conveyor selector switch, and photographs were examined by a third party engineering firm. The engineering firm report did not mention any deficiencies in the limit switch'. The conveyor control switch that controls the forward motion of the pipe on the inside conveyor system was found to be heavily worn and dirty and to stick in the forward position, which could cause uncontrolled pipe movement under certain conditions. The independent investigation by Allseas also found that there were no defects in the operation of the limit switch', and that the conveyor control switch would occasionally stick in the forward position.

Based on the results of the examination of the controls, it is not likely that the limit switch malfunctioned allowing the pipe joints on the conveyor to move. It is possible that a malfunction of the conveyor control switch contributed to the accident. However, if the limit switch were functioning properly, they would have prevented the pipe joints from moving, once they were engaged, even if the conveyor control switch malfunctioned. Therefore, a malfunctioning conveyor control switch by itself could not have caused the accident. The fact that RR5 had not become energized with CS1 could be attributed to a malfunction in the control system. However, no evidence justifies this conclusion.

3)   Improper or Inadvertent Activation of Controls. As noted above, it is most likely that the limit switch' were working properly. Therefore, in order for the pipe joints to move, the limit switch' would have had to be improperly or inadvertently defeated at the same time

30

that the pipe on the inside conveyor was energized forward. It is unlikely that the RBMO energized the conveyor (either by operating the conveyor selector switch or by operating the override button) while working in the gap between the pipe joints. The control console was approximately 8 feet away from the work area and, therefore, not within reach by the RBMO. Interviews with the crew indicated that, at the time of the accident, no one else was seen in the area that could have activated the controls.

As noted earlier, if the walking beam is used to lift the pipe joint at RR5 while the other joints on the conveyor system are advanced, it is possible to be disengaged from both RR5 limit switches. Limit Switch 1 is disengaged when the pipe joint in position RR5 is lifted approximately 2.5 centimeters off rollers by the walking beam. In this situation, limit switch-2 would not be engaged, which would allow the pipe on the inside conveyor to move forward if the conveyor system were energized by the conveyor switch being stuck in the forward position. The walking beam could have been inadvertently lifted by the RBMO. There was a make shift joystick extension on the walking beam control at knee level. This control stick could have been inadvertently nudged enough to elevate the walking beam.

The walking beam may have been inadvertently elevated while the seam rotator operations were being conducted. Since the seam rotator is controlled by the Bow Bevel Machine Operator, the RBMO could have been working in the gap between the pipe joints when the Bow Bevel Machine Operator lowered the seam rotator rollers. As the seam rotator limit switch-2 was closed, assuming the conveyor switch malfunctioned by sticking in the forward position, the conveyor could have been energized while the RBMO was in the gap between the pipe joints.

Contributing Causes

1) Inadequate hazard analyses and failure to implement hazard analysis recommendations was a contributing cause of the accident. In one of the hazard analyses reviewed by the panel, the recommendation for a barrier to prevent personnel from entering between the pipe prep area and the conveyor was not identified until after the accident. Thus the panel concludes that this hazard analysis was inadequate at the time of the accident. Although the BMO's were not specifically identified as persons at risk in this hazard analysis, the equipment and operations listed in the analysis appear to be those related to BMO tasks.

31

Another hazard analysis that specifically mentions the BMO's as persons at risk, identified recommendations for: 1) barriers at incoming pipe conveyors and 2) no buffing works on the incoming pipe conveyor. These recommendations were not implemented until a month after the accident. From documentation of this hazard analysis, the panel could not determine whether or not an analysis of this hazard had been conducted before the accident. If this analysis had not been conducted before the accident, then the hazard analysis specifically applicable to the BMO's was inadequate (non-existent). If this hazard analysis did exist before the accident and did not include the two recommendations noted above, then that hazard analysis was in adequate to prevent the RBMO from being caught between pipe joints. If this hazard analysis did exist before the accident and did include the two recommendations noted above, then that hazard analysis was not adequately implemented since there was no barrier where the RBMO was working at the time of the accident.

In addition, although CCTV cameras were installed in the ready rack area, as recommended by Allseas' hazards analyses, they were not working the day of the accident. Routine observation of activities in the ready rack area by foremen or supervisors might have identified unsafe work practices, malfunctioning equipment, or even the need to install a barrier. It is not known why the cameras were not working on the day of the accident.

The inadequacy of the hazard analyses and failure to implement them was especially critical since the hazards analyses indicated that exposure to these hazards was a daily occurrence with the severity, possibly resulting in an injury, dismemberment, or fatality. The safety of the RBMO relied heavily on personnel behavioral precautions and procedures noted in the JSA (see item 2 below). The only significant physical/mechanical barrier in the area where the RBMO was working was the Limit Switches (limit switch's). There was no back up for the possible failure or improper operation of one or both of these switches. If a physical barrier had been installed where the RMBO was working, at the time of the accident, the fatality most likely would have been prevented.

2) Failure to adequately implement and adhere to the JSA was a contributing cause of the accident. Although the JSA's indicated that personnel should not walk between pipe joints, the RBMO's hand grinder was stored on a bracket on a wall such that the RBMO had to walk between the pipe joints to obtain the hand grinder. The team determined that the RBMO had already gotten his hand grinder and had started to use it when the accident occurred. However, the fact that RBMO

would have likely walked between the pipe joints to get his hand grinder, perhaps several times in one shift, may have reinforced the unsafe behavior of working in this pinch point.

The RBMO failure to adhere to the following recommendations in the JSA:
- Don't walk between pipes. Go under pipe, not between pipe.
- Stand to the side of the pipe while grinding.

Although the RBMO had to walk between the pipe joints to get his hand grinder, he could have conducted the actual grinding by standing on the side of the pipe, as recommended in the JSA. If he had stood on the side of the pipe while grinding, he would have most likely seen the pipe on the conveyor begin to move and gotten out of the way, thus avoiding a serious injury.

3) The inadequacy of the JSA was a contributing cause of the accident. Job tasks were often vague rather than specific. The JSA also did not include important steps in the task sequence, and did not address the Bow Bevel Machine Operator and RBMO tasks individually. Both the Bow Bevel Machine Operator and RBMO had tasks to lift/move pipe. However, the JSA provided no information about how they would communicate and coordinate their tasks. In addition, the JSA did not adequately integrate the operation of the limit switch' into the task sequences.

4) Inadequate supervision was a contributing cause of the accident. Although the JSA indicated that personnel should not walk between pipe joints and should stand to the side of the pipe when grinding, interviews with crew members indicated that it was routine for personnel to walk between and work between the pipe joints. The panel could find no evidence that supervisors, who were routinely in the area on a daily or weekly basis, requested or required the crew to cease this practice.

5) Lack of a detailed written job description and formal training for bevel machine operators was a contributing cause of the accident. If the tasks specific to moving and hand grinding pipe had been included, perhaps some additional attention or training would have been provided to ensure the safety of these operations.

6) Failure of the RBMO to attend safety meetings was a contributing cause of the accident. Attendance at safety meetings might have increased the RBMO's awareness of the hazards he was encountering on a daily basis.

7) Possible inadequate inspection/maintenance of the control panel switch was a contributing cause of the accident. None of the crew interviewed mentioned the sluggish action of the conveyor switch. However, Allseas and the third party engineering firm, that analyzed the limit and control panel switches after the accident, did find that the conveyor switch was sluggish and that it was dirty and cracked. This condition could indicate inadequate inspection/maintenance of the switch, although no maintenance guidelines were available for the panel to confirm this. It should also be noted that there is no conclusive evidence that proves the condition of the conveyor switch was a contributing factor to the accident.

Recommendations

The investigative panel recommends that MMS take the following actions:

- Publish a safety alert that describes the accident, outlines the causes, and recommends that Lessees/Operators take the actions listed below.
- Minerals Management Service inspections on pipelay vessels should continue to be diligent about looking for potential pinch points. Any deficiencies should be brought to the attention of the contractor and the lessee.

Recommendations for Lessees and Operators during pipelay operations:

- In addition to the safety barrier placed in the area where RBMO was crushed, more safety barriers should be placed around all exposed pinch point areas along the conveyor system to prevent personnel from also entering those hazardous areas.
- Warning signs should also be posted to alert personnel of pinch point areas.
- Supervisory observations should be conducted more frequently in order to monitor work habits of all personnel in all areas, in particular the bead stall areas.
- Lessees should review the company's safety meeting policies with contract personnel and express the importance of conducting safety meetings. The Lessees should also emphasize that documentation of all meetings, and those personnel in attendance, is required.
- Lessees should review the JSA with affiliated personnel relating to the pinch point areas and communication.
- Contractors should consider installing CCTV cameras in the bead stall and ready rack areas to allow vessel supervision to oversee operations.
- Contractor should provide detailed written job descriptions and implement formal training modules for specific job duties and responsibilities
- All safety equipment in place should be inspected for proper operation on each tour. Any inoperable equipment should be repaired or replaced immediately. Once replaced or repaired, all equipment must be tested for proper operation. Proper documentation of these test results should be required.

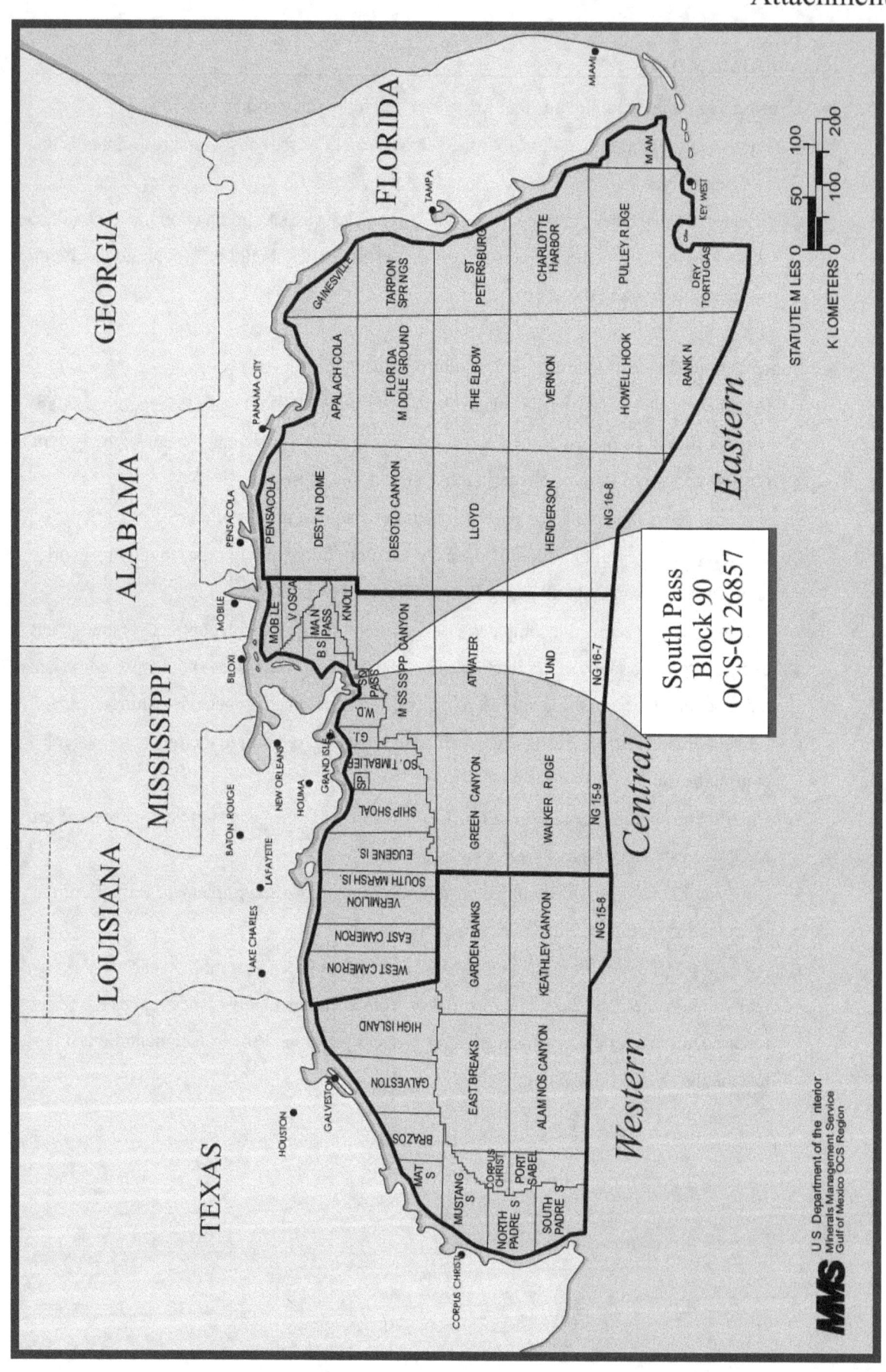

"Location of Right-of-Way OCS-G 26857, Block 90, South Pass, South and East Additions Area"

Aerial view of the Lorelay with pipe supply barge along side

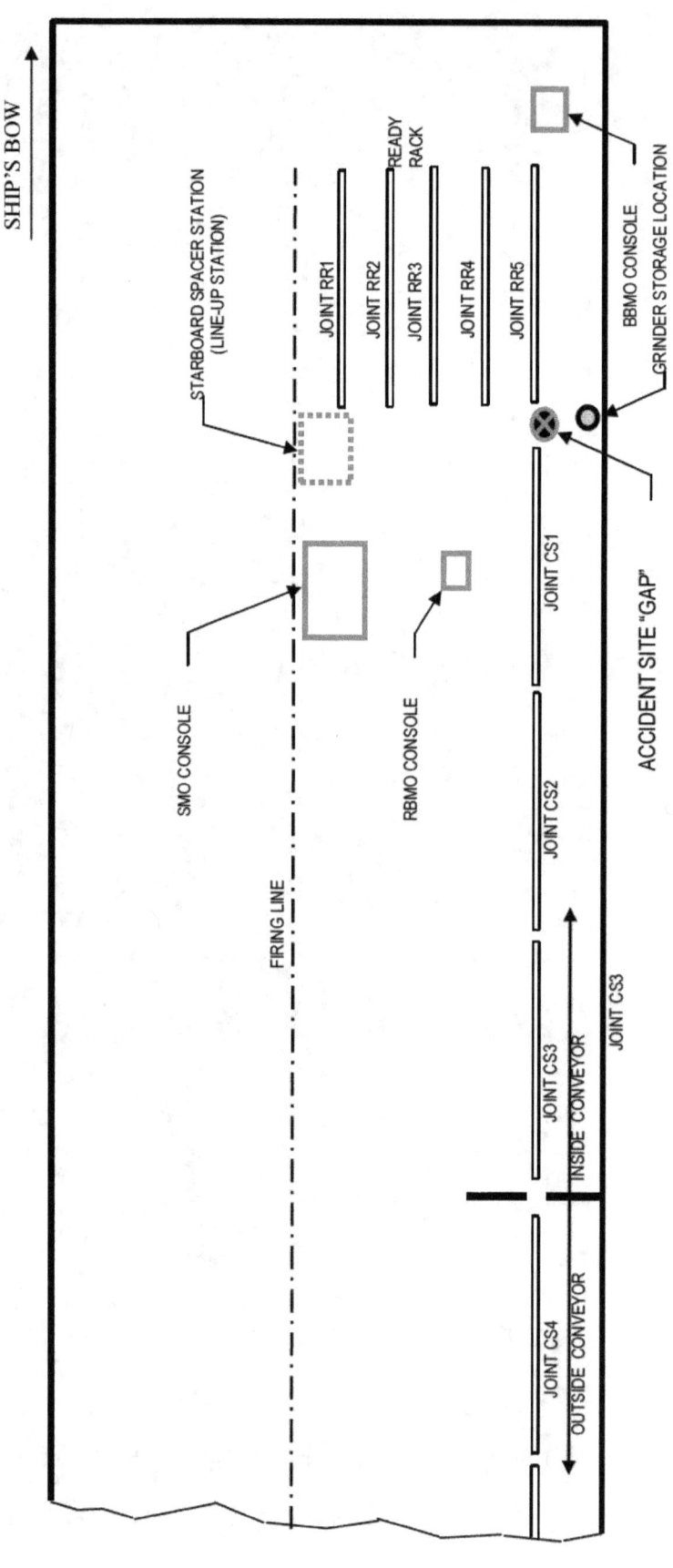

Configuration of the bead stall and ready rack areas at the time of the accident

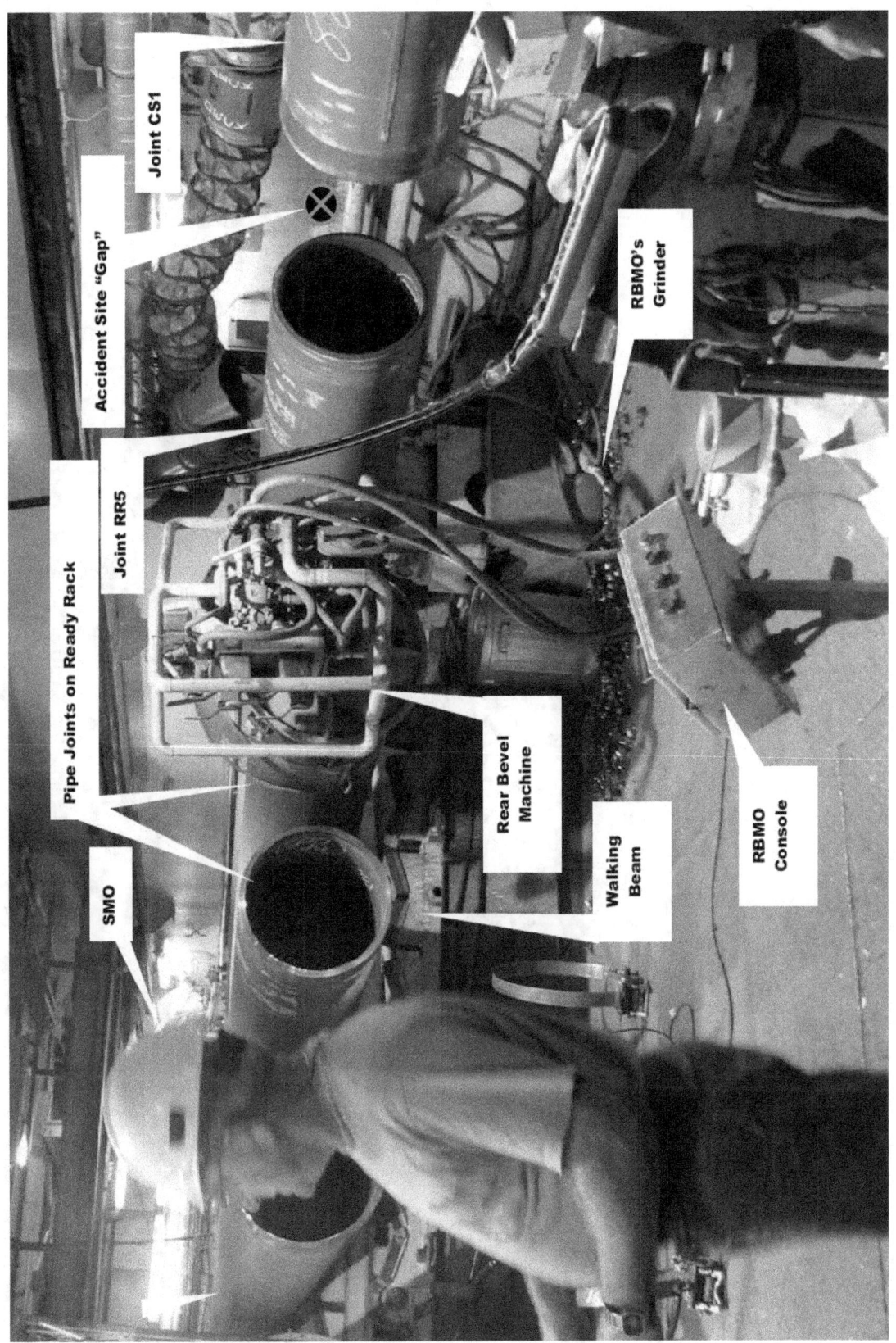

Accident Scene – Looking Toward Bow

Pipe Conveyor System – Looking Toward Stern

On-deck Pipe Storage Area and Outside Conveyor

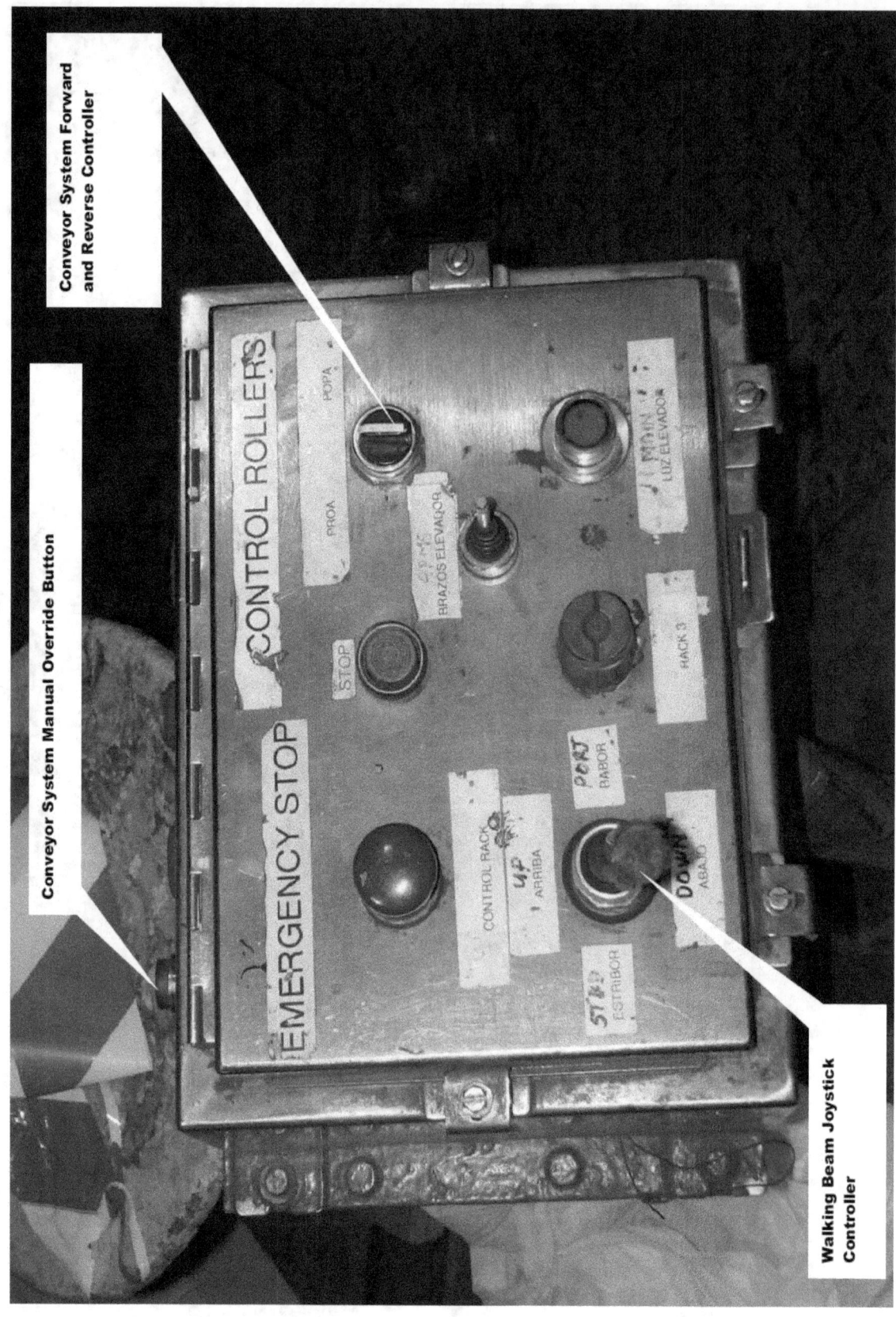

Rear Bevel Machine Operator (RBMO) Console – front view

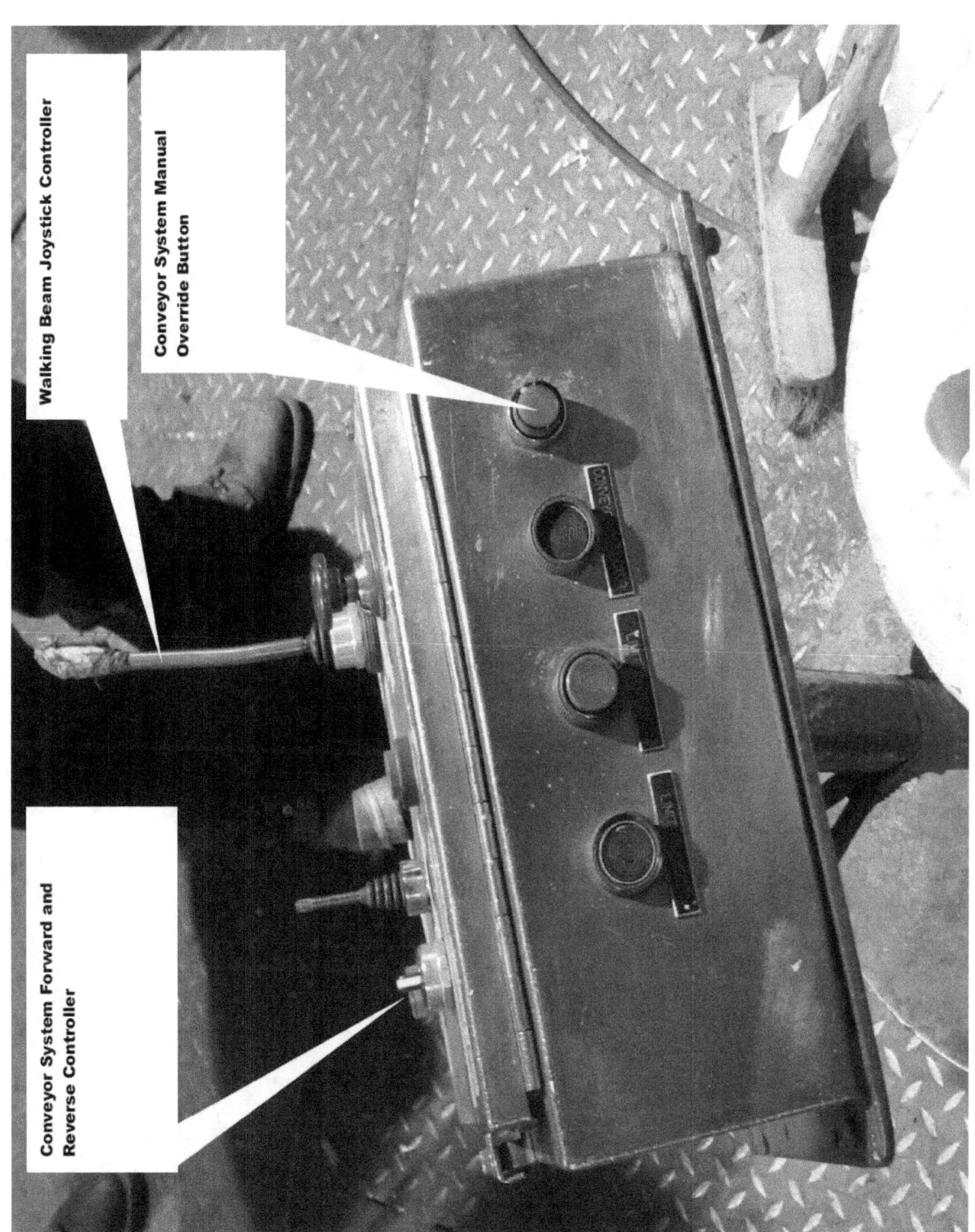

Walking Beam Joystick Controller

Conveyor System Manual Override Button

Conveyor System Forward and Reverse Controller

Rear Bevel Machine Operator (RBMO) Console – top view

www.ingramcontent.com/pod-product-compliance
Lightning Source LLC
Chambersburg PA
CBHW052018280526
45793CB00005B/1032